# Rookie Read-About® Science

# How Things Work:
# X-Ray Machines

by Joanne Mattern

**Content Consultant**
Eric Kearsley, Ph.D.
Volunteer, National Museum of American History
Smithsonian Institution

**Reading Consultant**
Jeanne M. Clidas, Ph.D.
Reading Specialist

**Children's Press®**
An Imprint of Scholastic Inc.

Library of Congress Cataloging-in-Publication Data
Mattern, Joanne, 1963- author.
  X-ray machines / by Joanne Mattern.
     pages cm. -- (Rookie read-about science. How things work)
  Summary: "Introduces the reader to x-ray machines."-- Provided by publisher.
  ISBN 978-0-531-21371-1 (library binding) -- ISBN 978-0-531-21459-6 (pbk.)  1.  X-rays--Juvenile literature.
2.  Medical radiology--Juvenile literature. 3.  Medical innovations--Juvenile literature. 4.  Discoveries in
science--Juvenile literature.  I. Title.

QC481.M44 2016
616.07'572--dc23                                    2015018075

Produced by Spooky Cheetah Press
Design by Keith Plechaty

Printed in China 62

SCHOLASTIC, CHILDREN'S PRESS, ROOKIE READ-ABOUT®, and associated logos are trademarks and/or
registered trademarks of Scholastic Inc.

1 2 3 4 5 6 7 8 9 10 R 25 24 23 22 21 20 19 18 17 16

Photographs ©: cover: Nick Veasey/Getty Images; 3 top left: Konstantin Shevtsov/Shutterstock, Inc.; 3 top
right: itsmejust/Shutterstock, Inc.; 3 bottom: Bork/Shutterstock, Inc.; 4: Yuganov Konstantin/Shutterstock,
Inc.; 7: Akawath/Shutterstock, Inc.; 8 main: wavebreakmedia/Shutterstock, Inc.; 8 inset: Yagi Studio/
Exactostock-1527/Superstock, Inc.; 11: warioman/Thinkstock; 12: Digital Vision/Thinkstock; 15: Science Photo
Library/Media Bakery; 19: njgphoto/iStockphoto; 20 top left: DV/Media Bakery; 20 top right: anankkml/
iStockphoto; 20 bottom left: The Natural History Museum/Alamy Images; 20 bottom right: Ted Kinsman/
Science Source; 23: Jeff Kowalsky/EPA/Newscom; 24 main: Seth Resnick/Superstock, Inc.; 24 inset:
DawidKasza/iStockphoto; 26 top: Bettmann/Corbis Images; 26 bottom: Album/Prisma/Superstock, Inc.; 26-
27 center: Martin Capek/Shutterstock, Inc.; 27 top: Dragon Images/Shutterstock, Inc.; 27 bottom: TJPhotos/
Alamy Images; 30 top: Alexander Tsiaras/Science Source; 30 bottom: Alexander Tsiaras/Science Source;
31 top: Westersoe/Thinkstock; 31 center top: Dragon Images/Shutterstock, Inc. 31 center bottom: Science
Photo Library/Media Bakery; 31 bottom: Jupiterimages/Thinkstock.

Illustrations by Jeffrey Chandler/Art Gecko Studios!

# Table of Contents

A doctor shows a patient an X-ray of her hip bones.

# Looking Inside

Imagine you could look inside your body and see all your bones. You can—with an X-ray machine.

An X-ray machine is used to make pictures of your bones.

Can you tell which bones are broken? ▶

The pictures an X-ray machine makes are usually called "X-rays."

An X-ray is a tool doctors use. It helps them see if a bone is hurt or broken.

## FUN FACT!

Getting an X-ray can be helpful. But getting too many X-rays can make a person sick. That is why doctors use them very carefully.

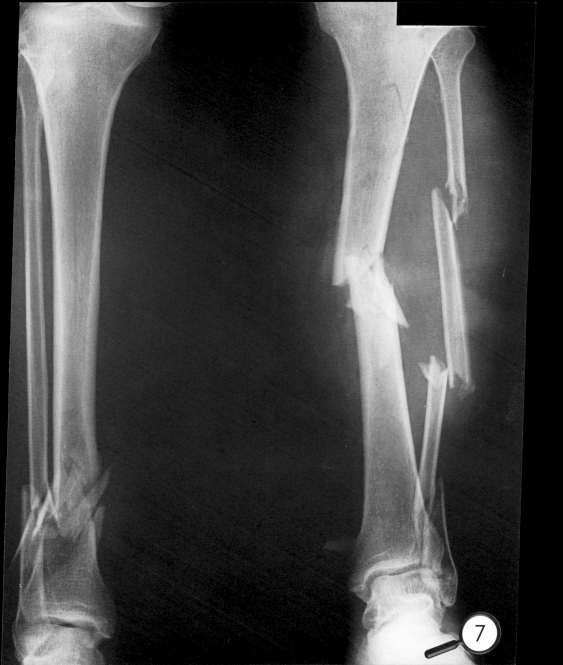

7

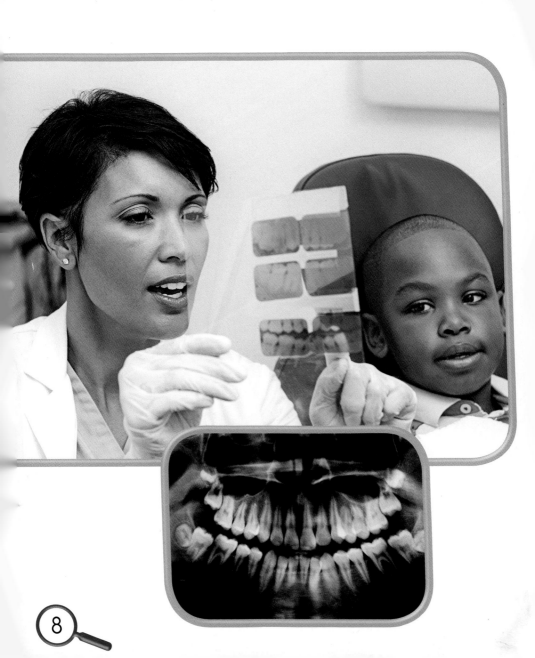

You may have had an X-ray picture taken at the dentist. Your teeth are bones. The dentist can use an X-ray machine to check for cavities.

# X-Rays Are a Kind of Light

To understand how an X-ray machine works, you need to understand light.

The light we can see is called visible light. It cannot pass through objects, including your body.

X-ray light is another kind of light.

When something blocks visible light, it makes a shadow.

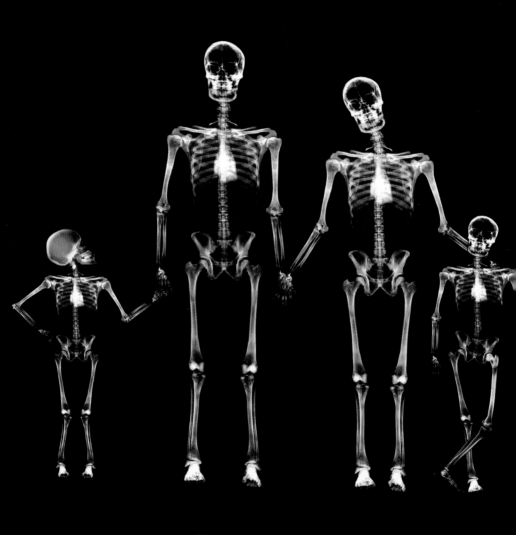

This X-ray shows every bone in the human body.

X-rays are not visible. They are more powerful than visible light. X-rays can shine through objects. They can pass through almost everything in your body. That includes your skin, blood, and muscles.

It is not as easy for X-rays to pass through bones. The thicker the bone is, the harder it is for X-rays to pass through it. That is the secret to how an X-ray machine works.

# How Does It Work?

Say you hurt your arm and the doctor wants to see the bone. A medical **technician** will take an X-ray. He or she will use an X-ray machine. An X-ray machine is like a camera. It uses a special kind of film.

The X-ray film is inside the container under the girl's arm.

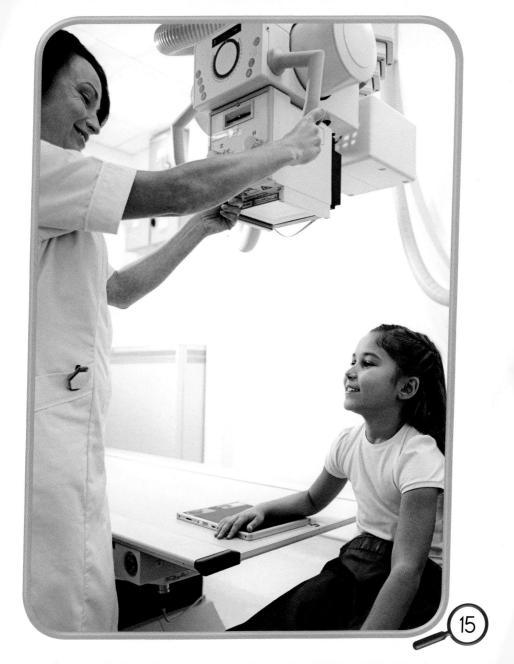

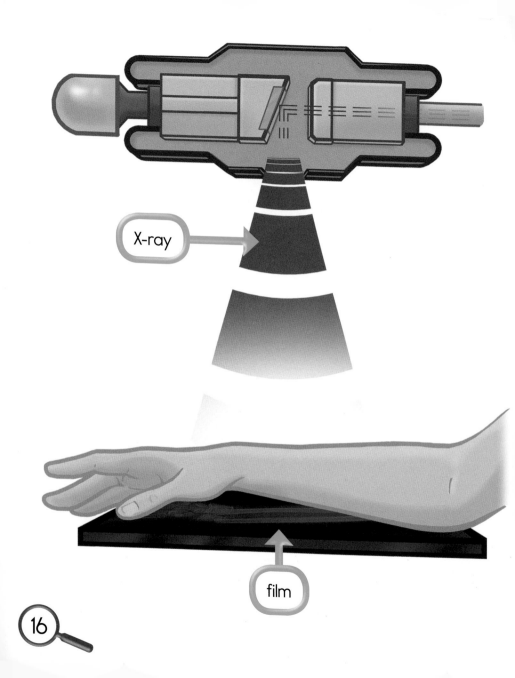

X-ray

film

16

First you put your arm on the film. This is where the picture will show up. Then the machine shines X-ray light on your arm. The X-ray light goes through your arm and shines onto the film.

When you get an X-ray, it does not hurt. You cannot feel X-rays!

But remember, X-rays cannot go through bone. The bone blocks the X-ray light from hitting the film. So your bones show up on the film in white.

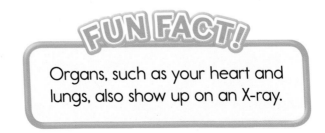

**FUN FACT!**

Organs, such as your heart and lungs, also show up on an X-ray.

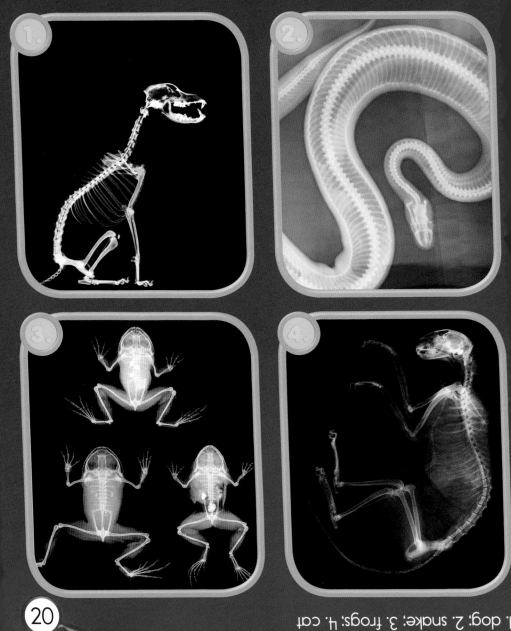

1. dog; 2. snake; 3. frogs; 4. cat

# Who Else Uses X-Rays?

**Veterinarians** sometimes use X-rays to look at the bones of an animal.

Check out these animal X-rays. Can you tell what kinds of animals they are by looking at their bones?

Taking an X-ray of a large animal can be tricky. The animal must stay very still while the picture is taken.

Zoo elephants get trained just for this. They are taught to place a foot on the X-ray equipment and stay perfectly still.

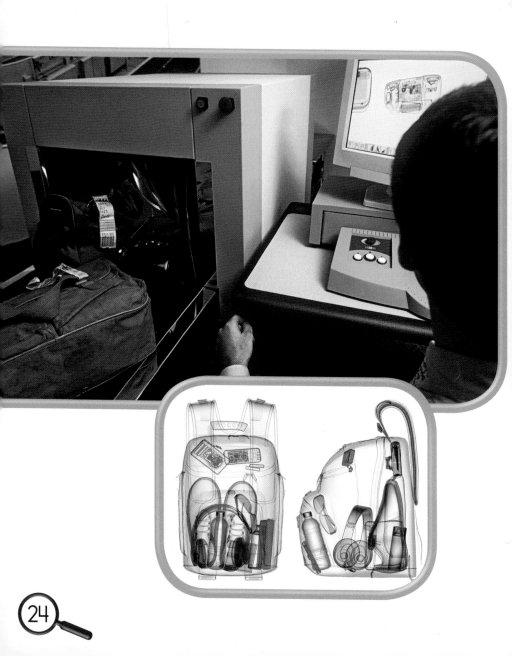

At airports, luggage is X-rayed. That is done to make sure nothing dangerous is inside.

Now you know how X-ray machines work. They give us a look into a whole other world!

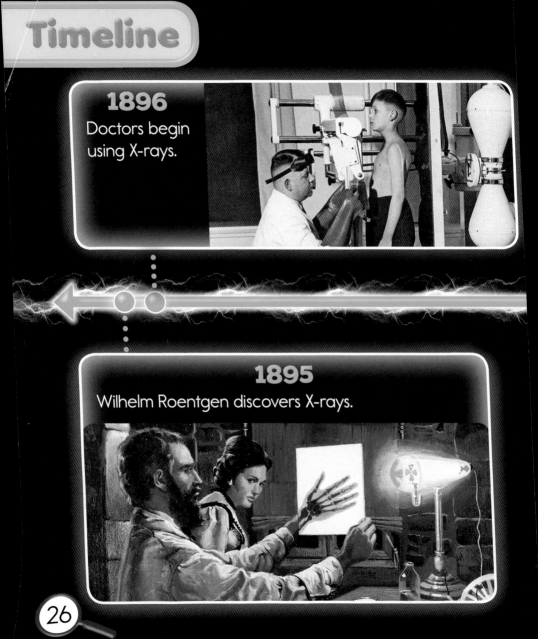

**1896**
Doctors begin using X-rays.

**1895**
Wilhelm Roentgen discovers X-rays.

## 1997

**Digital** X-rays are introduced. These machines do not use X-ray film. The X-ray image goes right to a computer screen.

## 1975

The CT scan is invented. The machine makes it easier for doctors to get a good look at a patient's organs. Here is a CT scan of a person's brain.

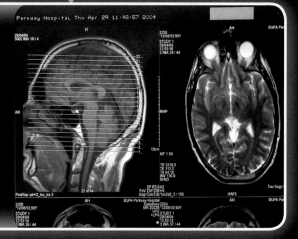

**Ask an adult for help. Do not attempt this science experiment on your own!**

X-rays can be dangerous, so it is not possible to do an experiment with them at home. This experiment shows you how X-rays work, without any of the danger!

**You Will Need:** Cardboard box (a shirt box is a good size), window screen, piece of cardboard, scissors, sand

**1.**

Place the window screen on top of the box.

**2.**

Use the scissors to cut a simple pattern, such as a star, a diamond, or a circle, out of the piece of cardboard.

**3.** Place the pattern on top of the screen.

**4.** Pour sand over the screen, including over the pattern. Remove the screen and look in the box. What do you see?

## Why This Works:

The sand passed through the screen just like X-rays pass through your body. However, the sand did not pass through the cardboard pattern. That is why you see an image of the pattern in the sand inside the box. In the same way, X-rays cannot pass through bones. Instead, they create an image of the bones on the X-ray film.

A CT machine is a different type of X-ray machine. An X-ray shows an outline of bones and organs in your body. A CT scan creates a digital three-dimensional image of your insides. That allows technicians to see a much clearer picture.

**Archaeologists** use CT machines to look at things from the past. This lets them see inside an object, such as a mummy's case (below), without destroying it.

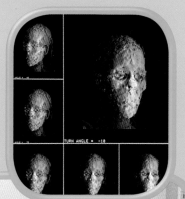

# Glossary

**archaeologists** (ar-kee-AH-luh-jists): people who learn about the past by studying old buildings and objects

**digital** (dij-uh-tuhl): produced as an image on a computer, without using film

**technician** (tek-NISH-uhn): person who works with specialized equipment

**veterinarians** (vet-ur-ih-NER-ee-uhns): animal doctors

# Index

# Facts for Now

Visit this Scholastic Web site for more information on X-ray machines:
**www.factsfornow.scholastic.com**
Enter the keywords **X-Ray Machines**

# About the Author

Joanne Mattern is the author of many nonfiction books for children. Science is one of her favorite subjects to write about! She lives in New York State with her husband, four children, and numerous pets.